DEAR VINCENT

Poems about Famous Paintings and Artists

Lucy Ann Linney

KDP

Copyright © 2020 Lucy Ann Linney

All rights reserved

No part of this book may be reproduced, or stored in a retrieval system, or transmitted in any form or by any means, electronic, mechanical, photocopying, recording, or otherwise, without express written permission of the publisher.

ISBN-13: 9798594065475

CONTENTS

Title Page	1
Copyright	2
Introduction	5
JACQUES and NAPOLEON	7
CRAGGY ROCKS	12
P R B	15
YOUTHFUL BEAUTY	18
COMING HOME	22
PRIDE OF LONDON	26
DOTS	29
DEAR VINCENT	33
ODYSSEUS! WHAT HAVE YOU DONE?	37
A MEXICAN TIGER! IS THAT TRUE?	40
I SPY FOXES	45
MISTER COLOUR	49
Acknowledgement	53
About The Author	55
Books By This Author	57

INTRODUCTION

As I write these poems, I am continually in awe of the artists and their creations. Some artists like Vincent Van Gogh and Henri Rousseau died penniless, never knowing how admired their art would become.

Others, like Dante Gabriel Rossetti and Sir John Everett Millais had vitriolic criticism levelled against them, as did Georges Seurat and Henri Rousseau.

Franz Marc and August Macke died too young in WW1. Who knows what other masterpieces they might have produced.

The story of how the people of Scotland contributed towards the £4 million needed to buy Sir Edwin Landseer's painting, Monarch of the Glen, is inspirational.

John William Waterhouse's painting is all about Ulysses and his thrilling adventures, whereas the enigmatic and brilliant Jacques Louis David was the ultimate political artist.

But whatever the story, I've chosen paintings that resonate with me. Maybe that's all art should have to do.

Dedication:
To all my grandchildren, I love you all.

JACQUES AND NAPOLEON

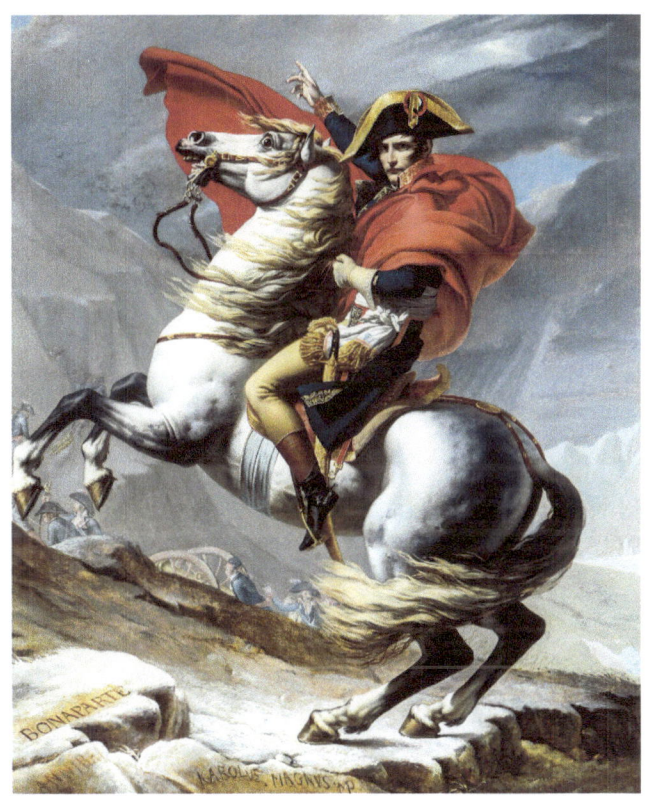

Artist: Jacques Louis David 1748 -1825

Painting: Napoleon Crossing the Alps 1802

Held at the Chateau de Malmaison, France

"I love your neoclassic style
and you're the one I need
to paint a portraiture of me
upon a fiery steed.

The trek across the Alps,
like Hannibal and Charlemagne,
will curry public favour
and boost my next campaign.

I have no time to sit and pose,
I'm such a busy man,
but here are all the funds you need,
so do the best you can."

Jacques Louis David's life
had been anything but quiet;
pivotal in France's reign
of terror, death and riot.

La Guillotine loomed darkly
over every cul de sac.
Jacques David, weren't you frightened
to go headlong down this track?

Jacques worked on propaganda
for a new public regime.
His metaphoric artwork
showed a viewpoint quite extreme.

A coup to paint this Corsican,
though David used his son
to pose on library ladders
'til the masterpiece was done!

Red for revolution!
Cloak flapping magically!
A clear symbolic battle cry,
shouts, "Onward, follow me!"

How much these two great men
in a cruel and savage age,
changed the fortunes of a nation,
only history will gauge.

◆ ◆ ◆

*There is another painting
of Napoleon crossing the Alps
by Paul Delaroche in 1850.
Held at the Walker gallery in Liverpool*

*This time Napoleon is riding on a mule.
He wears a brown coat and looks cold and downcast as
he is led through mountainous snow.
It was not nearly so popular as the Jacques Louis David depiction.*

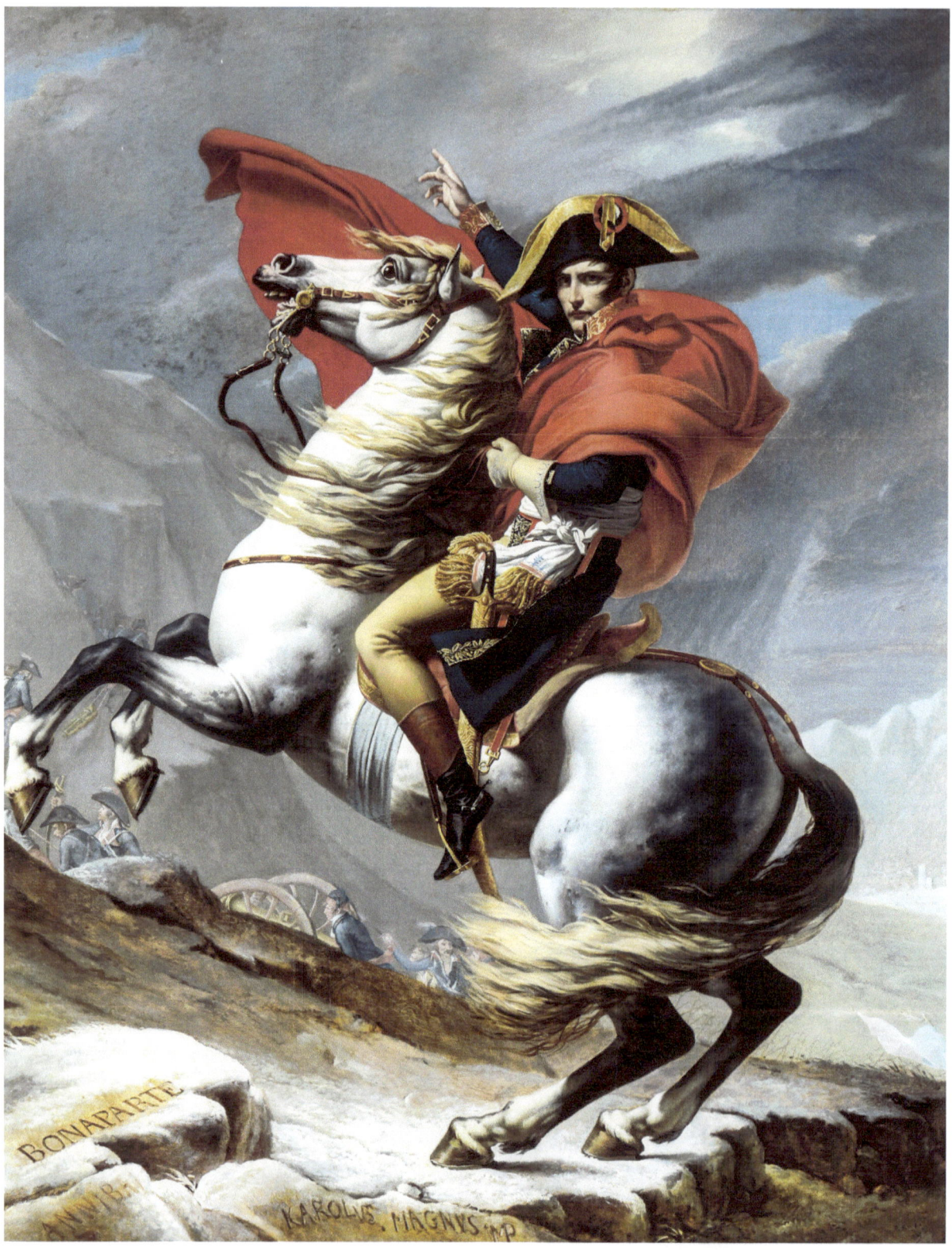

DEAR VINCENT

CRAGGY ROCKS

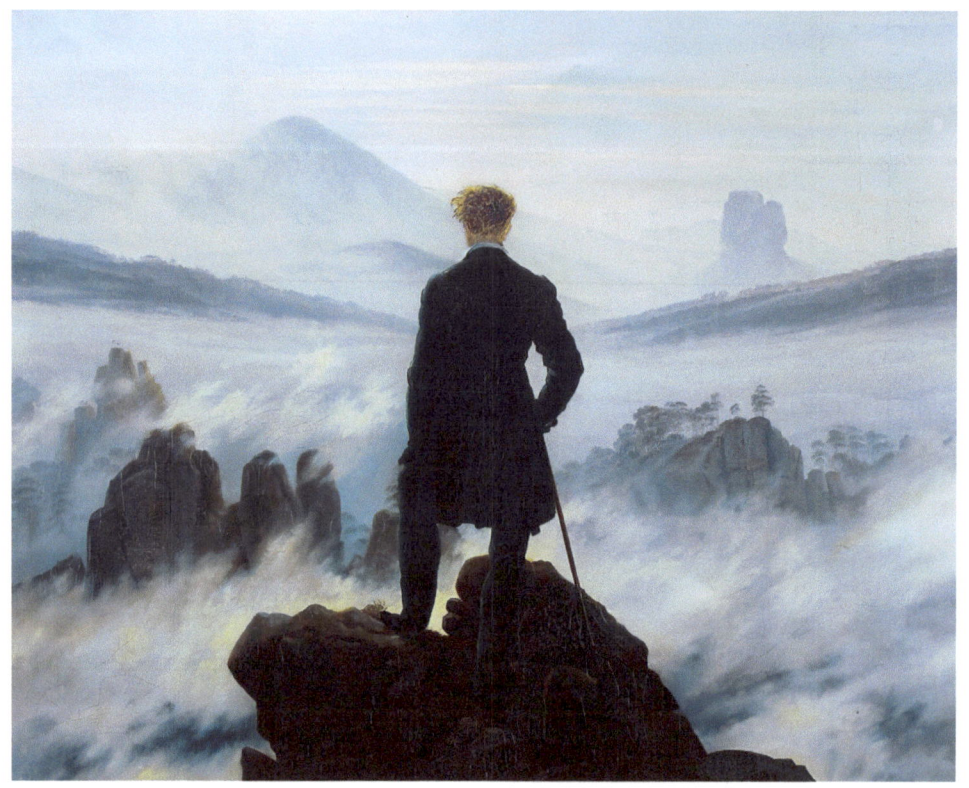

Artist: Casper David Fredrich 1774 -1840

Painting: Wanderer above the Sea Fog 1818

Held at Kunsthalle, Hamburg, Germany

Craggy rocks and mighty boulders,
a distant line of hidden trees
emerge from swirling, misty sea fog,
shifting in the morning breeze.

A haunting, landscape painting
that invites us in, but why
the fascinating interest in
this green clad, unique guy?

Just who was this wanderer,
poised with verve and flair,
sporting a Prussian army coat,
that a ranger might wear?

Standing firmly on high ground,
is he master of all he surveys,
or is he aware of man's fraility
in the face of nature's cool gaze?

As spectators, we stand behind him,
but imagine ourselves in his shoes,
staring out at distant horizons,
appraising his thoughts and his views.

LUCY ANN LINNEY

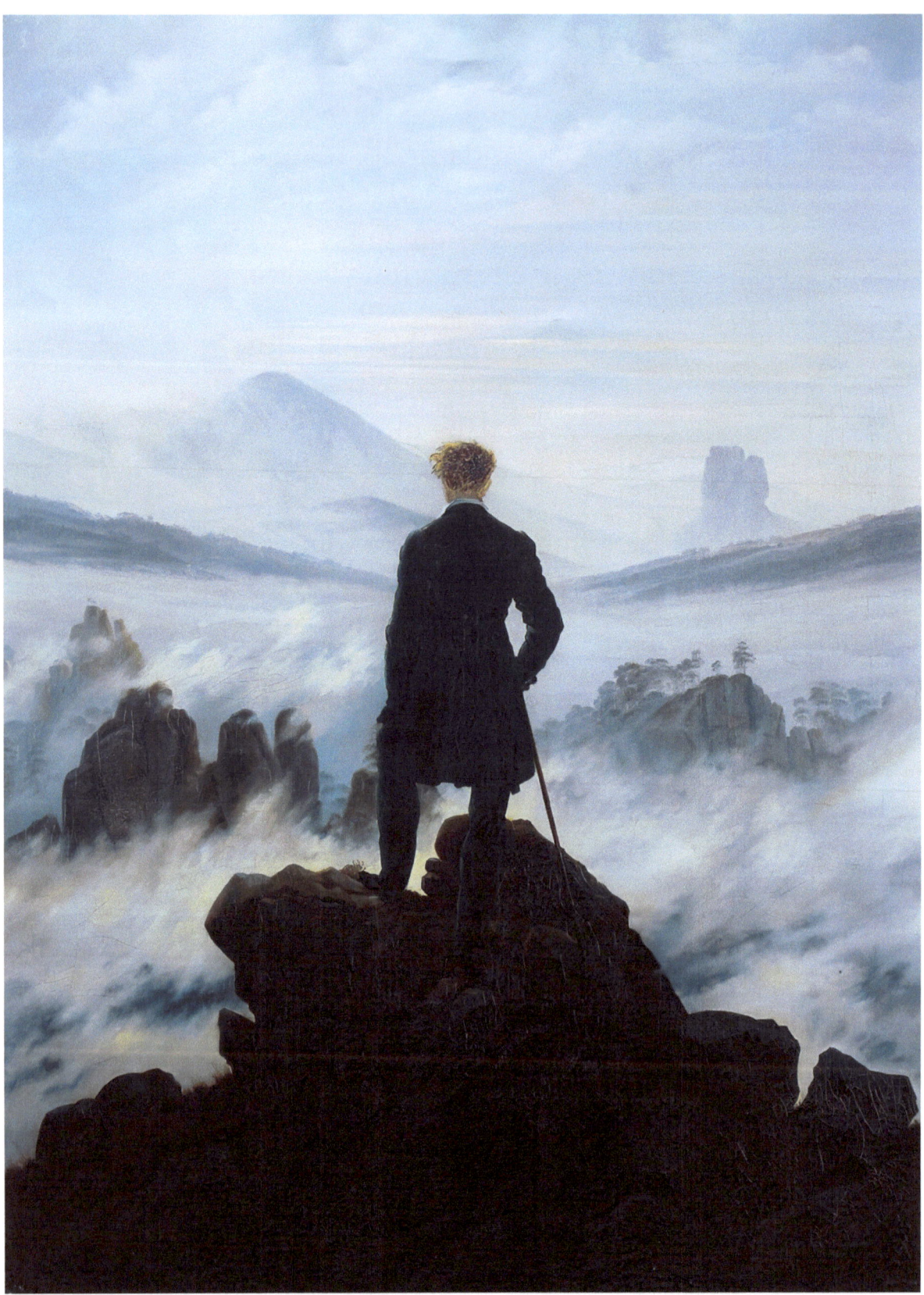

P R B
Pre- Raphaelite Brotherhood

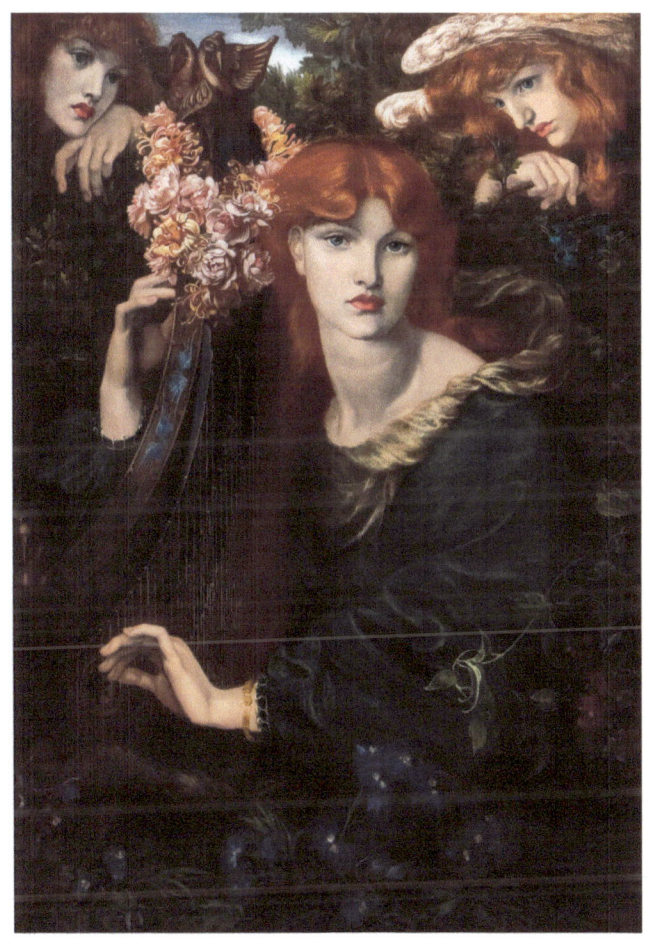

Artist: Dante Gabriel Rossetti 1828 -1882

Painting: La Ghirlandata 1873

Held at Guildhall Art Gallery, London

People started asking,
why the letters P R B
were written on exhibits
in the art Academy?
Outdated classic dogma
caused some young men to rebel.
They yearned for the lost freedoms
prior to Raphael.
They aimed to start anew,
by painting fables and religion,
weighted with emotion,
reality and vision.
Rossetti's women looked like
models in a magazine,
beautiful, aesthetic,
floral and serene.
The critics cried aloud,
"An attack upon the eye!
Too bright! Just not Victorian!
Too avant - garde! And why?
John Ruskin now spoke up in favour
of the brotherhood,
deciding that the new art style
was really rather good.

◆ ◆ ◆

John Ruskin 1819 - 1900
Victorian art critic

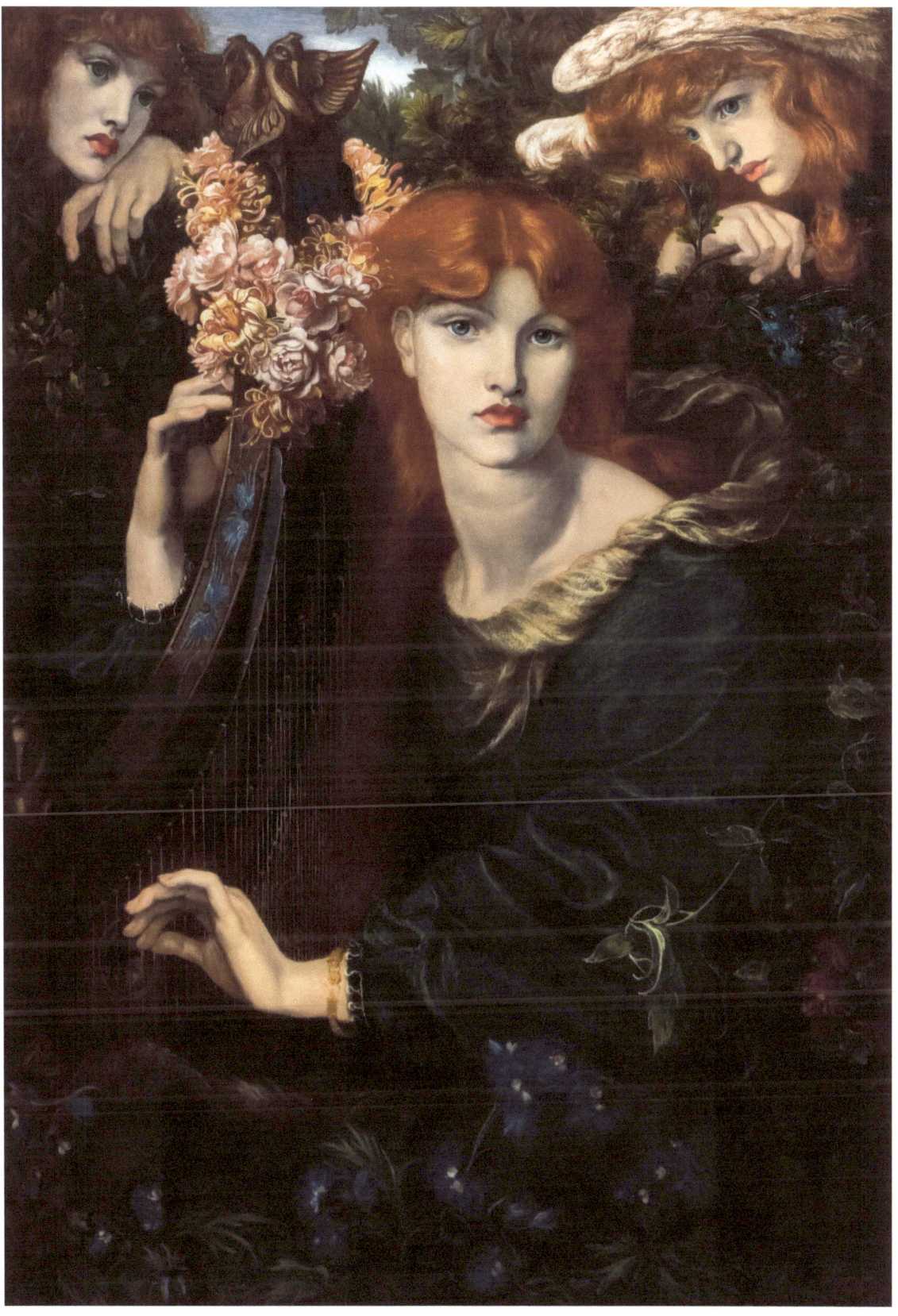

YOUTHFUL BEAUTY

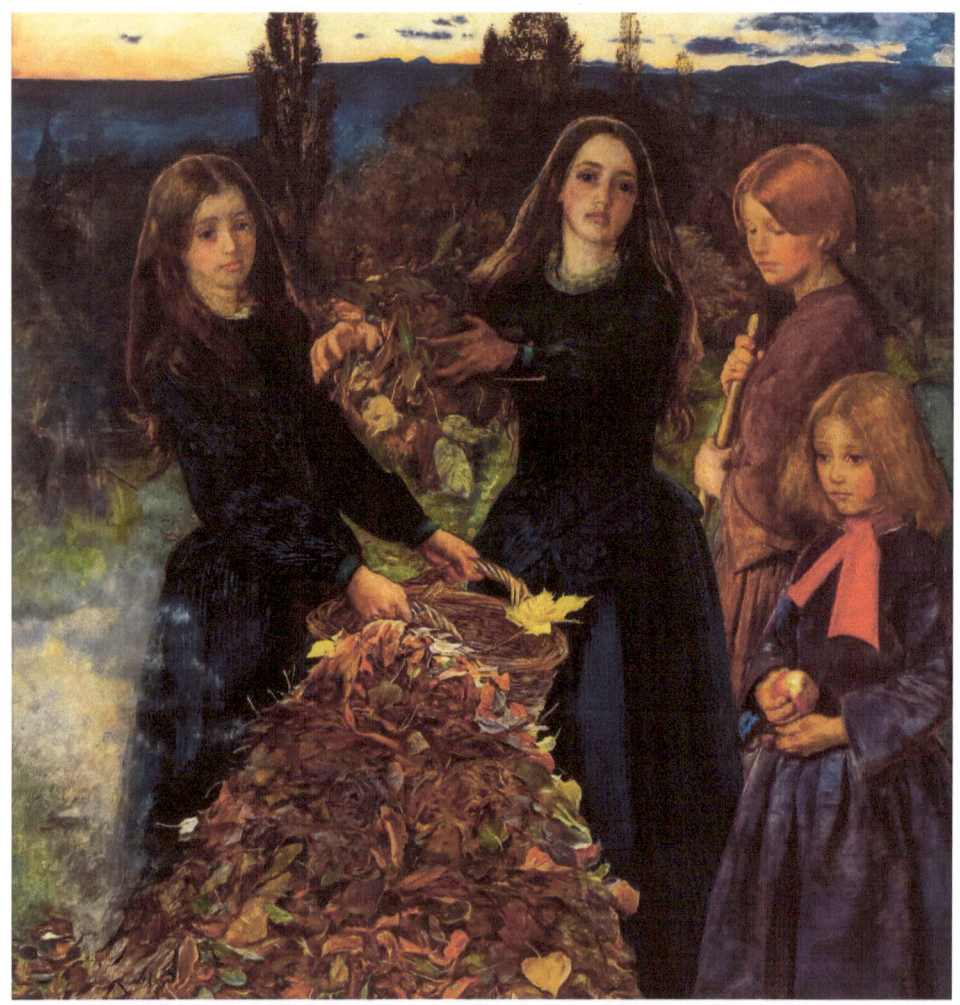

Artist: Sir John Everett Millais 1829 - 1896

Painting: Autumn Leaves 1856

Held at Manchester City Art Museum, Manchester

We meet, we greet
we say hello,
reading gestures
as we go!
Four wee lassies
work away,
but what do their
expressions say?

No merry making
or elation,
for laughter, there's
no inspiration.
Melancholy
pervades the air;
there's sadness
in a downturned stare.

The little child
has taken a bite
from the apple
that she's holding tight.
Surely! There's no
meaning base
in an action
so very commonplace?

The bonfire building
is quite exact,
leaves look rigid
and tightly packed.
Tiny curls of
smoke waft by,
heading for
the twilight sky.

Youthful beauty
can't be denied,
flawless in
the eventide.
Rustling leaves
of brown and green,
A memorable,
nostalgic scene.

◆ ◆ ◆

Members of the P R B
(The Pre-Raphaelite Brotherhood)

Dante Gabriel Rossetti 1828 - 1882
Sir John Everett Millais 1829 - 1896
Ford Maddox Brown 1821 -1893
William Holman Hunt 1827 - 1910

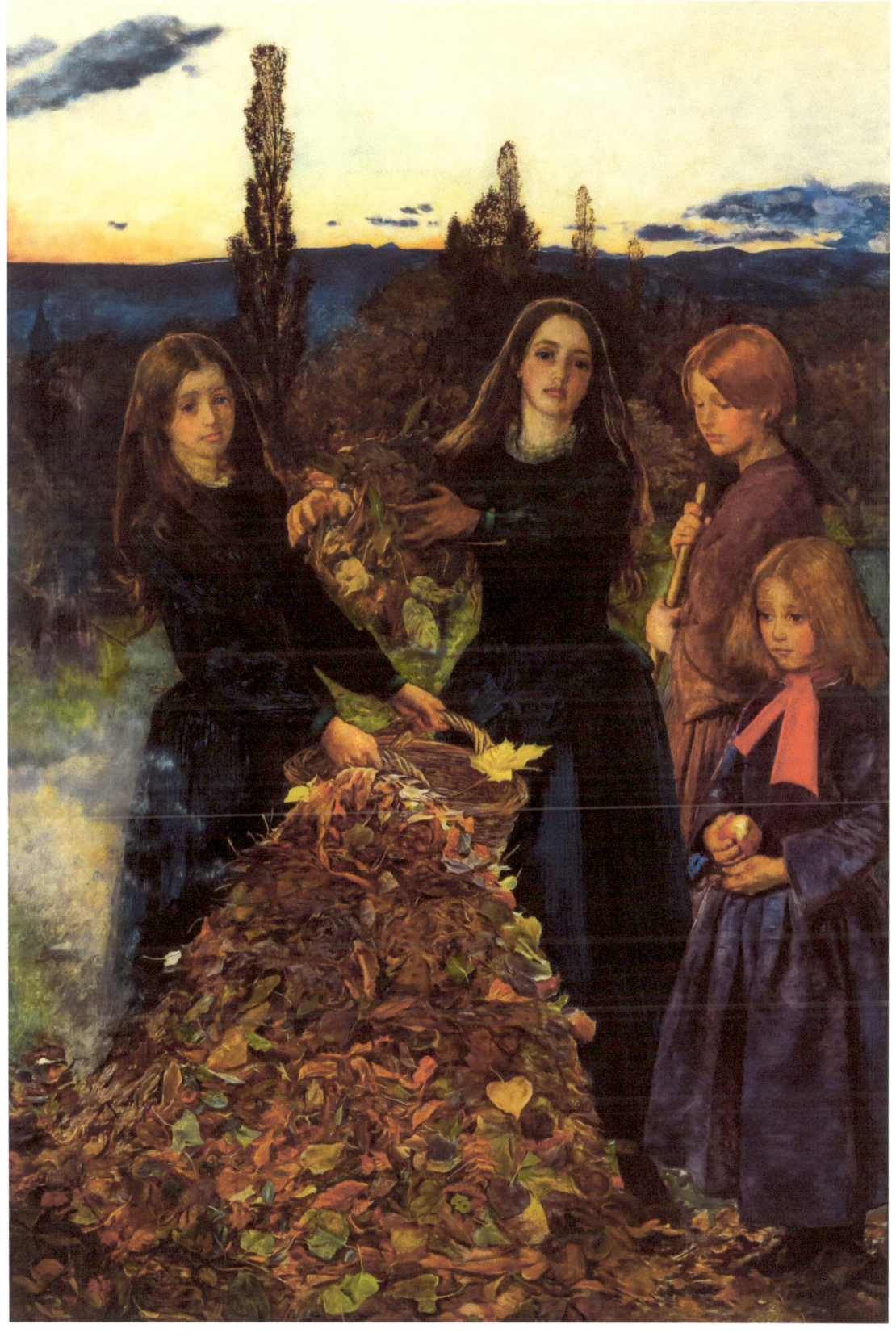

COMING HOME

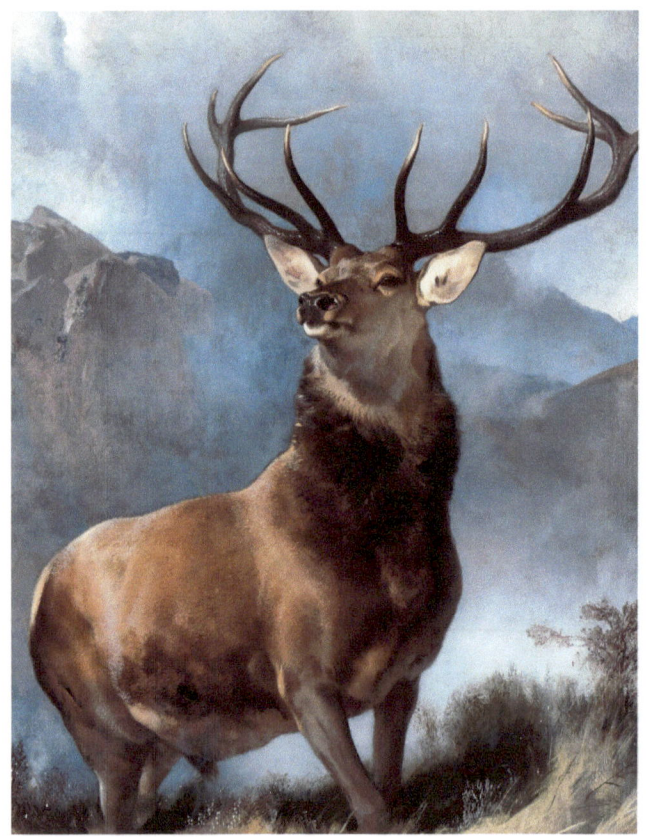

Artist: Sir Edwin Henry Landseer 1802 - 1873

Painting: The Monarch of the Glen 1851

Held at the Scottish National Gallery, Edinburgh

I'm only a stag, it's true,
without any right to fame,
and with four points short on my antlers,
I can't claim the monarch's name.
If you count the tines, there are twelve,
making me, a royal deer,
painted by the talented
and illustrious Landseer.
He caught my majestic nature,
powerful, noble, supreme.
Behold this honourable creature,
worthy of Scotland's esteem.
I'd been given the starring role
in a journey of highs and lows,
and with every twist and turn,
my reputation grows.
The great Palace of Westminster
was my first intended site,
but squabbles over money
meant this plan did not go right.
However, I was sold and put to work,
to be worth my salt;
advertising butter, shortbread,
soap and whisky malt...
but when another buyer came
to whisk me far away,
the dear people of Scotland
rallied round and let me stay.
I can't thank them enough
for their timely helping hand.
I find myself back where the mist
and heather daub the land.

LUCY ANN LINNEY

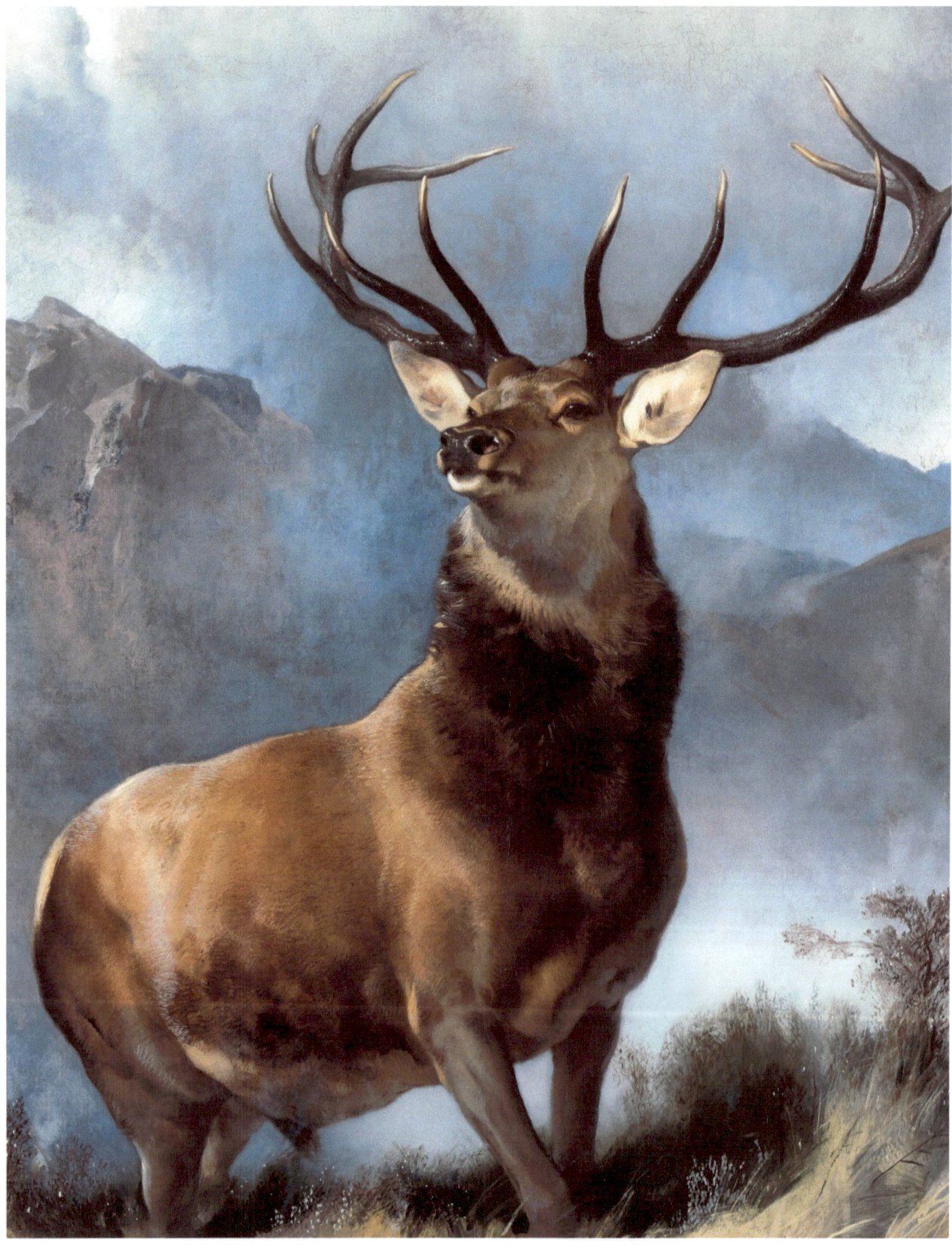

DEAR VINCENT

PRIDE OF LONDON

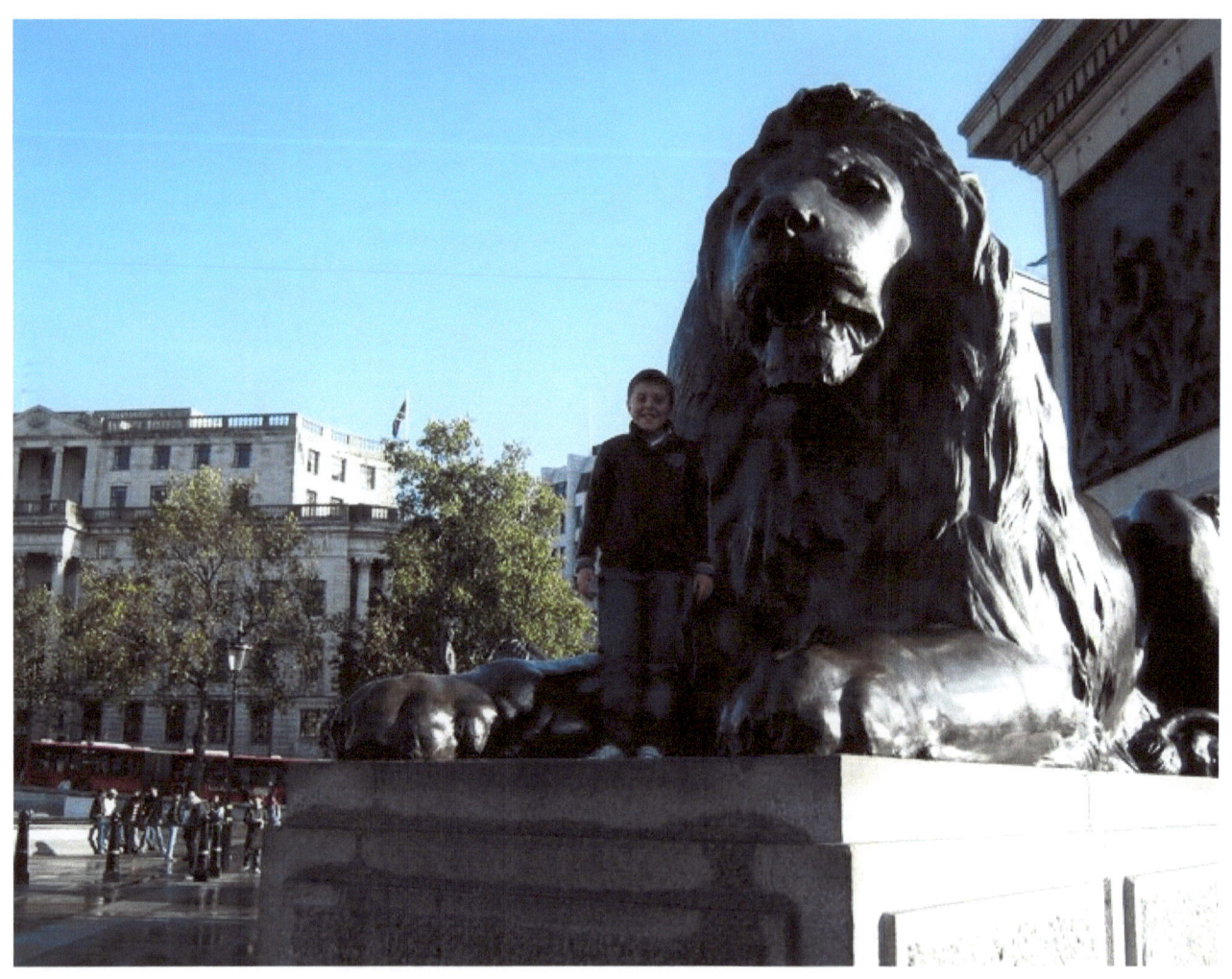

Sculptor: Sir Edwin Landseer 1802 -1873

Sculptures: The Lions of Trafalgar Square 1867

Did you feel the heavy burden,
was the task too much to bear;
that commission for the sculptures
of the lions in the square?
Eyebrows raised a tad, when others
heard you were the one
to use your skills at carving.
They muttered, "He has none!"
As Queen Victoria's favourite,
expectations would be high.
Your gift for painting animals
nobody could deny.
Ill health and doubt crept in,
no longer in your comfort zone.
For ten long years we waited,
while Lord Nelson stood alone.
With escalating costs,
did it ever cross your mind,
to disappoint the nation
and leave it all behind?
Why no! You persevered,
continued what you had begun;
bequeathing bronze creations
for generations still to come.
Demanding our respect,
sitting in awesome majesty,
behold the pride of London
in this famed locality.

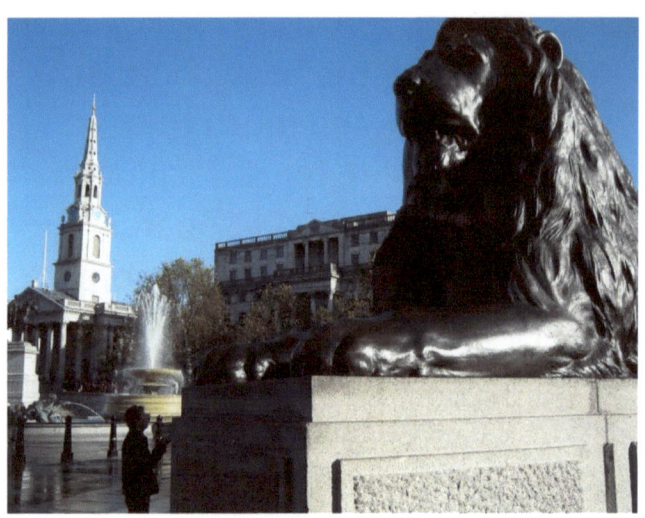

These photos were taken in 2009, when the sculptures had already been in situ for 142 years.
Harry aged 10 years

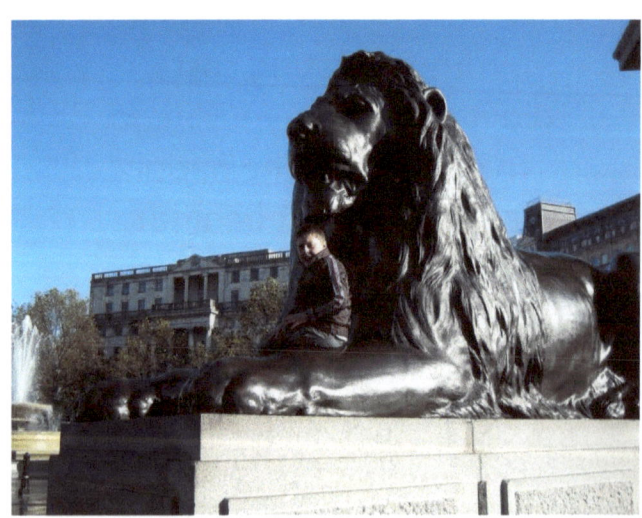

DOTS

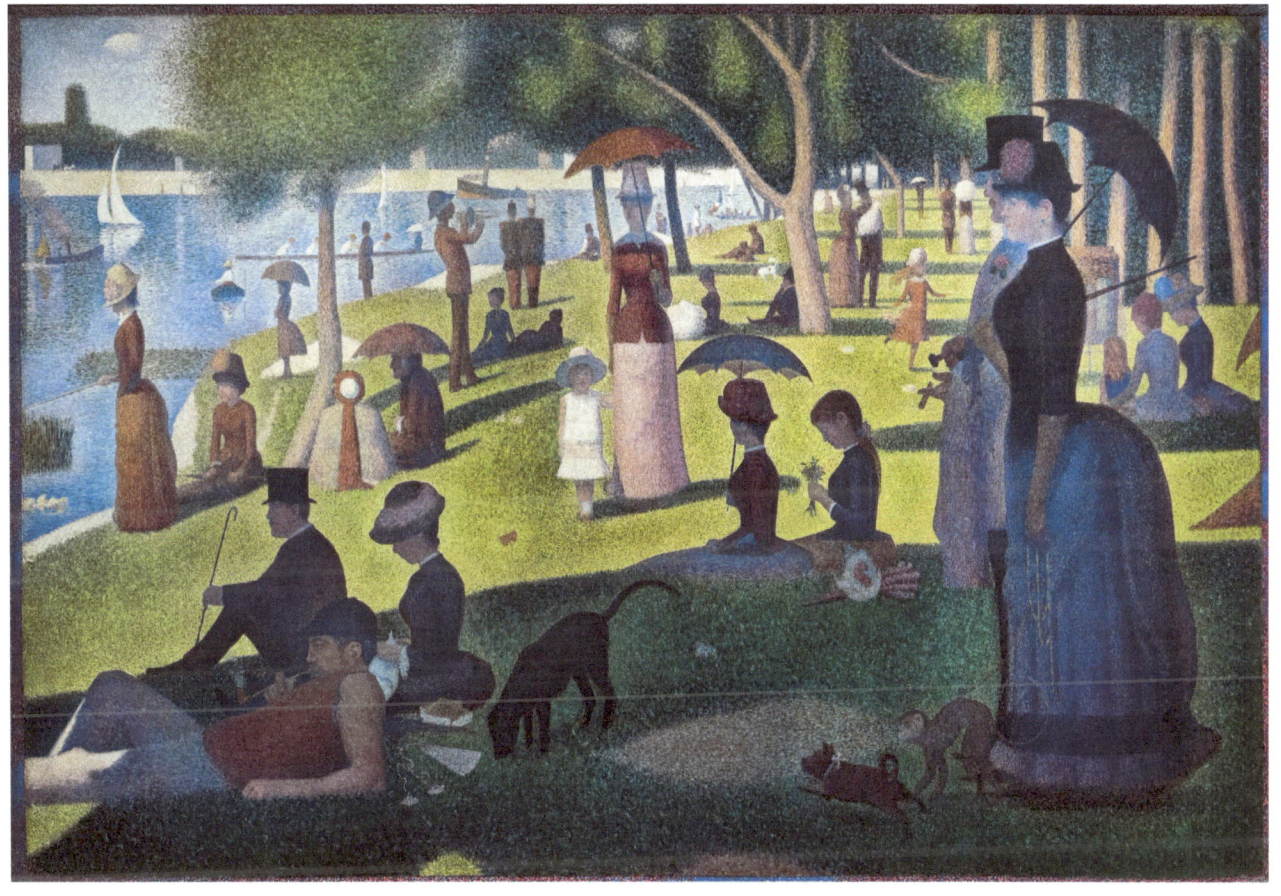

Artist: Georges Seurat 1859-1891

Painting: Sunday on La Grand Jatte 1886

Held at the Art Institute in Chicago

*Much larger than I thought,
it's an extraordinary endeavour,
utilising dots,
George Seurat was mighty clever.
Has anybody counted
every single little dot?
It must run into millions,
because there's lots and lots!
Sometimes there's space between
with the background coming through,
creating luminescence
from a pointillistic view.
Our eyes mix hues together.
How technical is that
when we stare at Seurat's masterpiece
Sunday on La grand Jatte?
This careful composition
was not a rushed affair.
He made so many sketches
with precision and great care.
Figures painted sideways
have a strong Egyptian feel,
portraying middle classes
as unchanging, bored, surreal.
Critics were quite flummoxed
citing, "Scandal!" in their view.
But with his fresh technique
Georges had devised something quite new.*

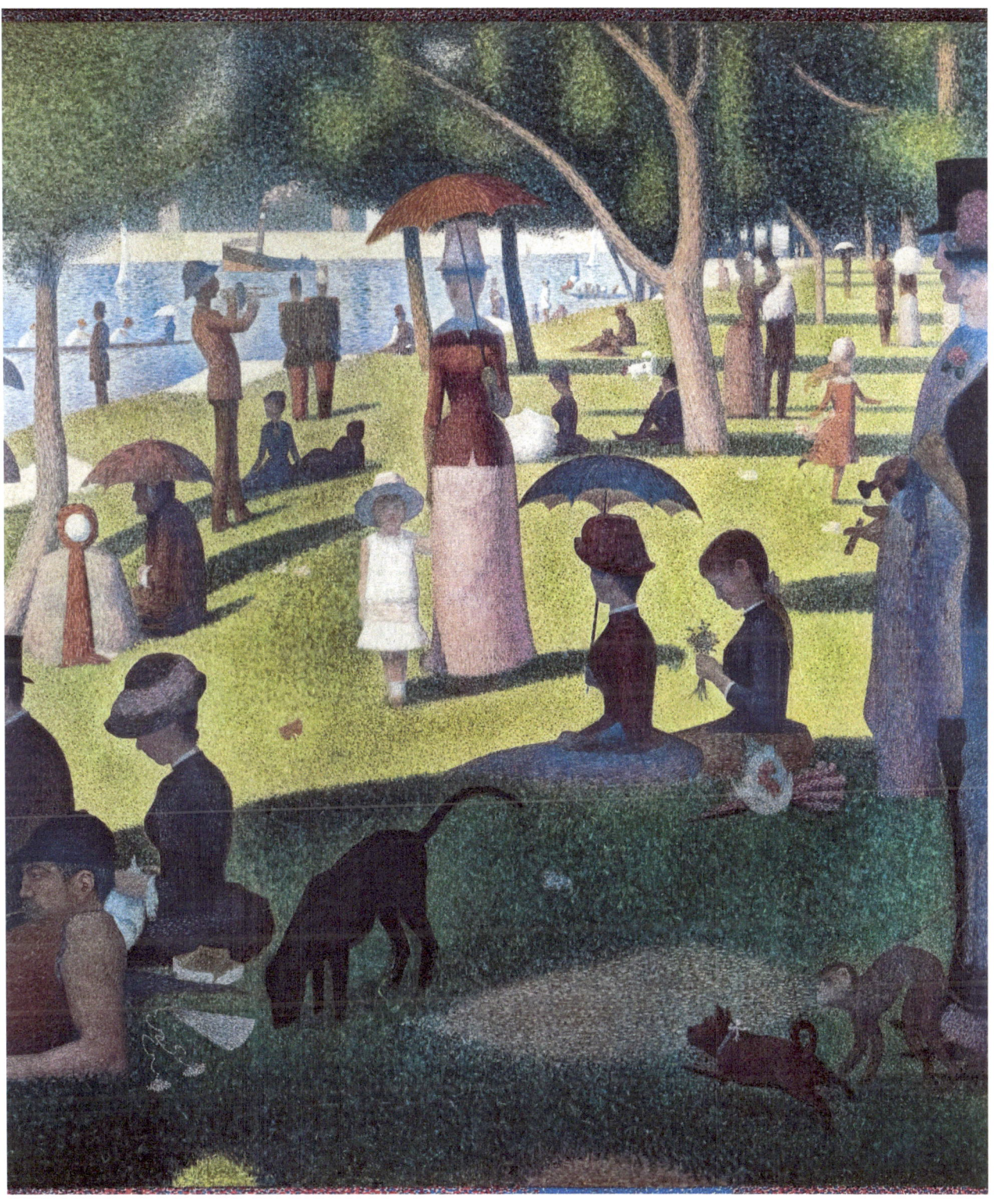

LUCY ANN LINNEY

DEAR VINCENT

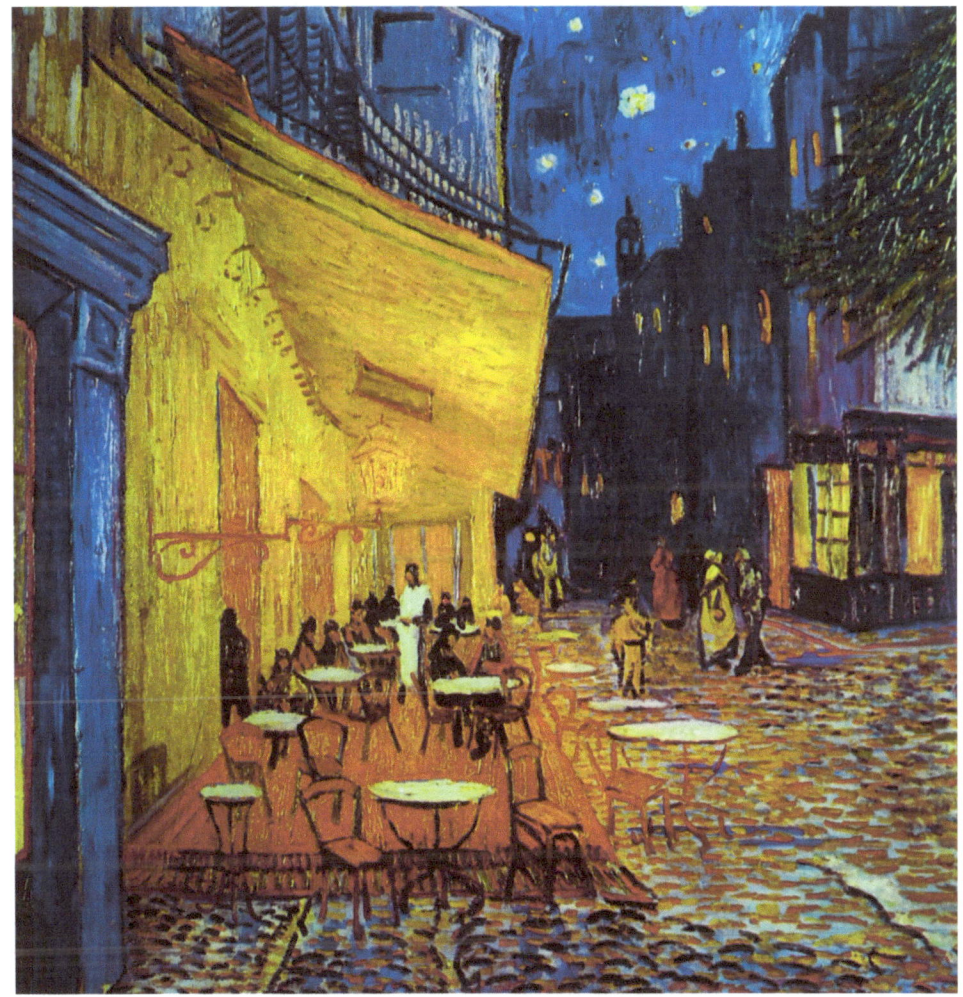

Artist: Vincent Van Gogh 1853 - 1890

Painting: The cafe Terrace at Night 1888

Held at the Kroller -Muller Museum, Otterlo. Netherlands

Epistles to your family have seen the test of time,
showing early passion for religion, books and art.
A restless, yearning, anguished soul, revealed upon the pages.
Were there signs of genius and madness from the start?

Your letter to your sister, both expressive and upbeat,
describes a fresh new picture that you painted in the night.
You talk of tiny figures sitting out upon the terrace,
with cafe front and pavement all immersed in yellow light.

The sky, that is your trademark, like nothing else we've seen
is decked with stars and nebulae in yellow, whitish hues.
You sound so happy that your palette has no trace of black;
instead there's purple, indigo and many other blues.

The street transforms from daytime grey to pinkish violet.
We could be in a discotheque, with flashing lights and swirls;
or shuffling through a fragrant heap of petals on the ground,
or searching on the ocean floor for abalones and pearls.

You loved to paint at night, it opened up a whole new phase.
It looked like you had found, at last, the perfect recipe.
You flourished in this climate of painting on the spot.
We're grateful for your paintings and for your legacy.

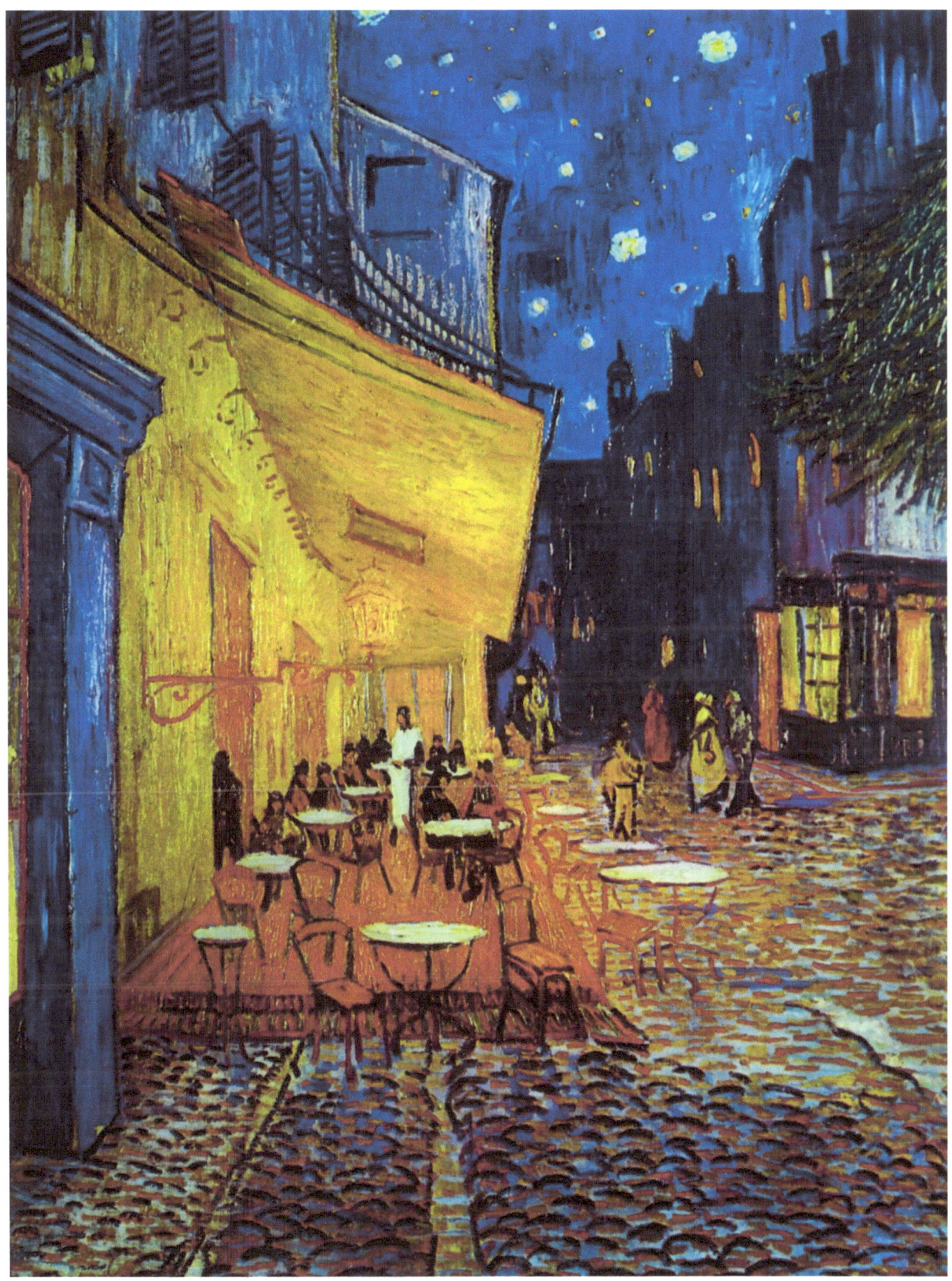

LUCY ANN LINNEY

ODYSSEUS! WHAT HAVE YOU DONE?

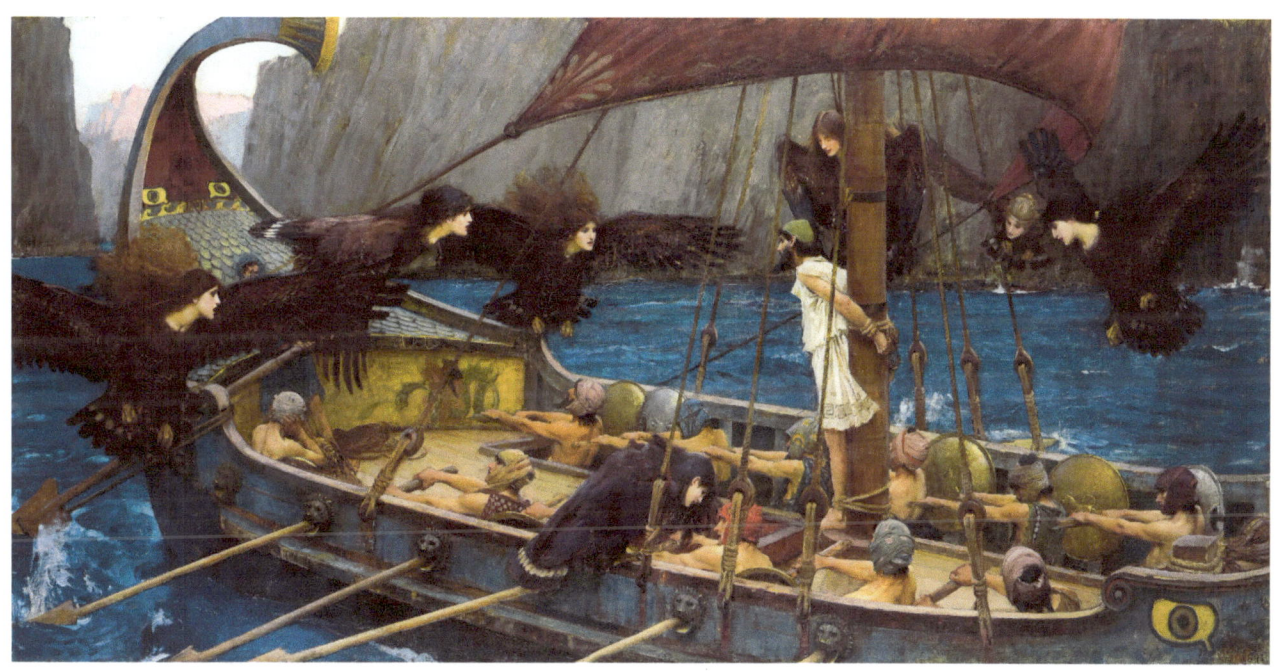

Artist: J. W. Waterhouse 1849-1917

Painting: Ulysses and the Sirens 1891

Held at the National Gallery of Victoria, Melbourne

Perched on the side of the galley,
the siren cooed with soft voice.
The oarsmen could not hear her
or else they'd have had no choice
but to follow the sweet singing temptress
back to her eerie, up where
the bones of others were scattered
and strewn in her green pastured lair.

Her beautiful face hid the talons
and black, vultured features so cruel.
Her sisters swarmed round feeling baffled.
Why were these oarsmen so cool?
With ears blocked with wax, the men rowed;
so the sirens focused at last
on the writhing, moaning sailor,
bound tight and secure to the mast.

It had been Odysseus' choice,
but on hearing each passionate plea, he blustered, swore and shouted,
"Untie these foul knots, release me!"
They somehow escaped with their lives,
no-one had done that before.
No doubt there'd be more adventures,
'til at last they arrived on home shore.

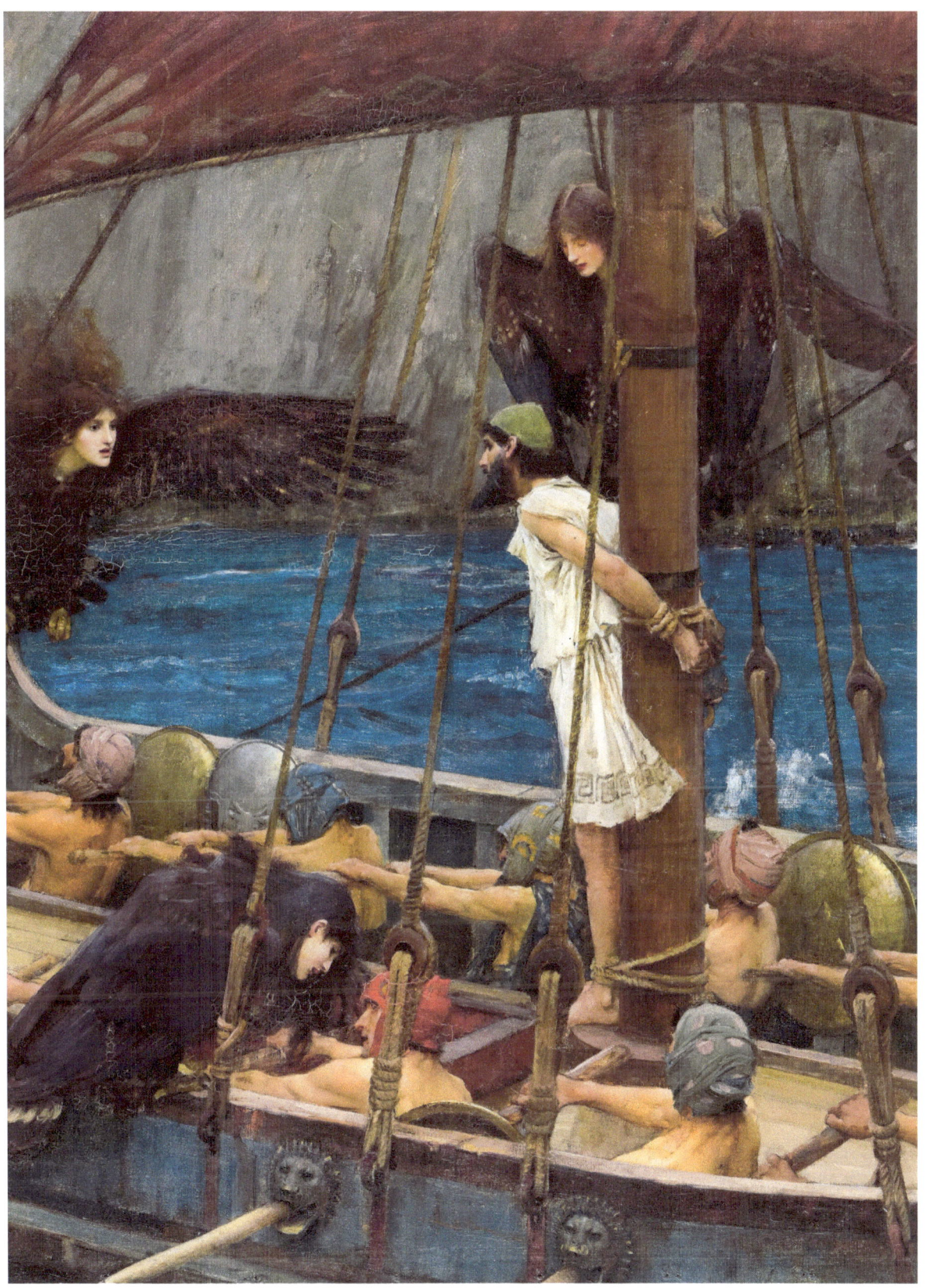

A MEXICAN TIGER! IS THAT TRUE?

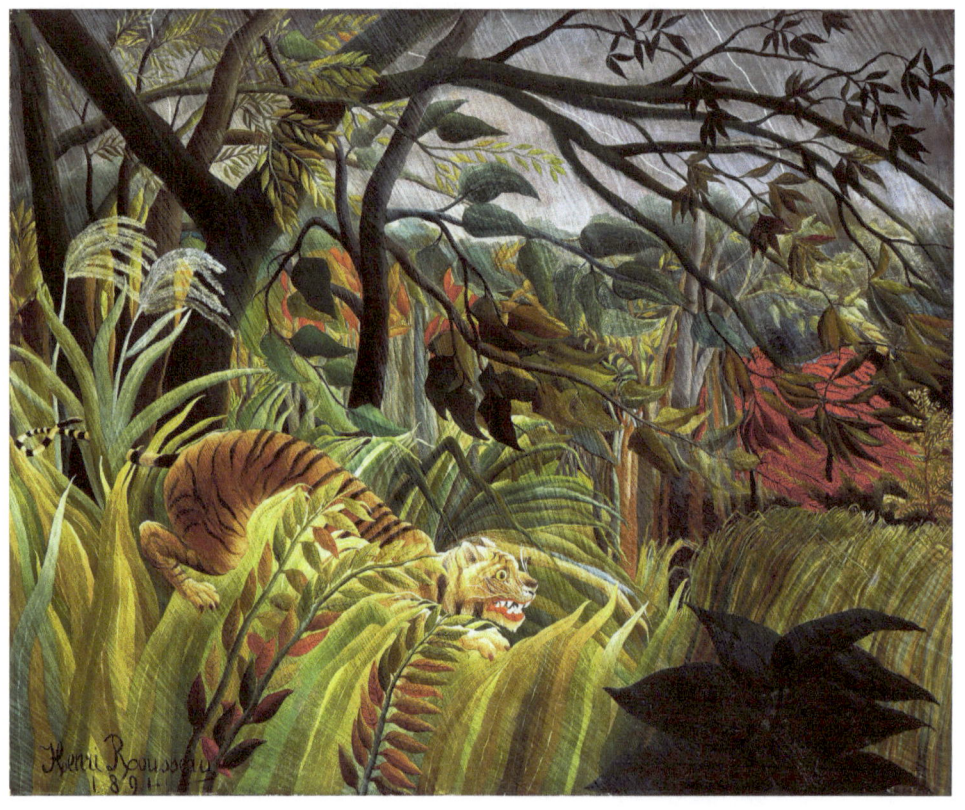

Artist: Henri Rousseau 1844 - 1910

Painting: Tiger in a Tropical Storm (Also called The Surprise) 1891

Held at The National Gallery, London

A tiger in a tropical storm
is eccentric and a strange art form.
What is the story? Give us a clue.
A Mexican tiger! Is that true?
That jungle tale has made me smile,
you've been in Paris all the while,
teaching yourself to paint and draw.
Your ambition is great,
but your talent is raw.
Rousseau had been on a mission
to show his work at The Exhibition.
The French committee all said, "No!
We're sorry, but you're not a pro.
Your style's naive, perspective wrong,
here at The Salon, you don't belong."
The artist thought he'd go elsewhere
to see how "The Surprise!" would fare.
Rousseau ignored the critic's view
and went independent for his debut.
How proud would Henri be today
to see his paintings on display
in galleries across the nation
feeding our imagination?
Henri's lesson has to be,
keep on going, that's the key.

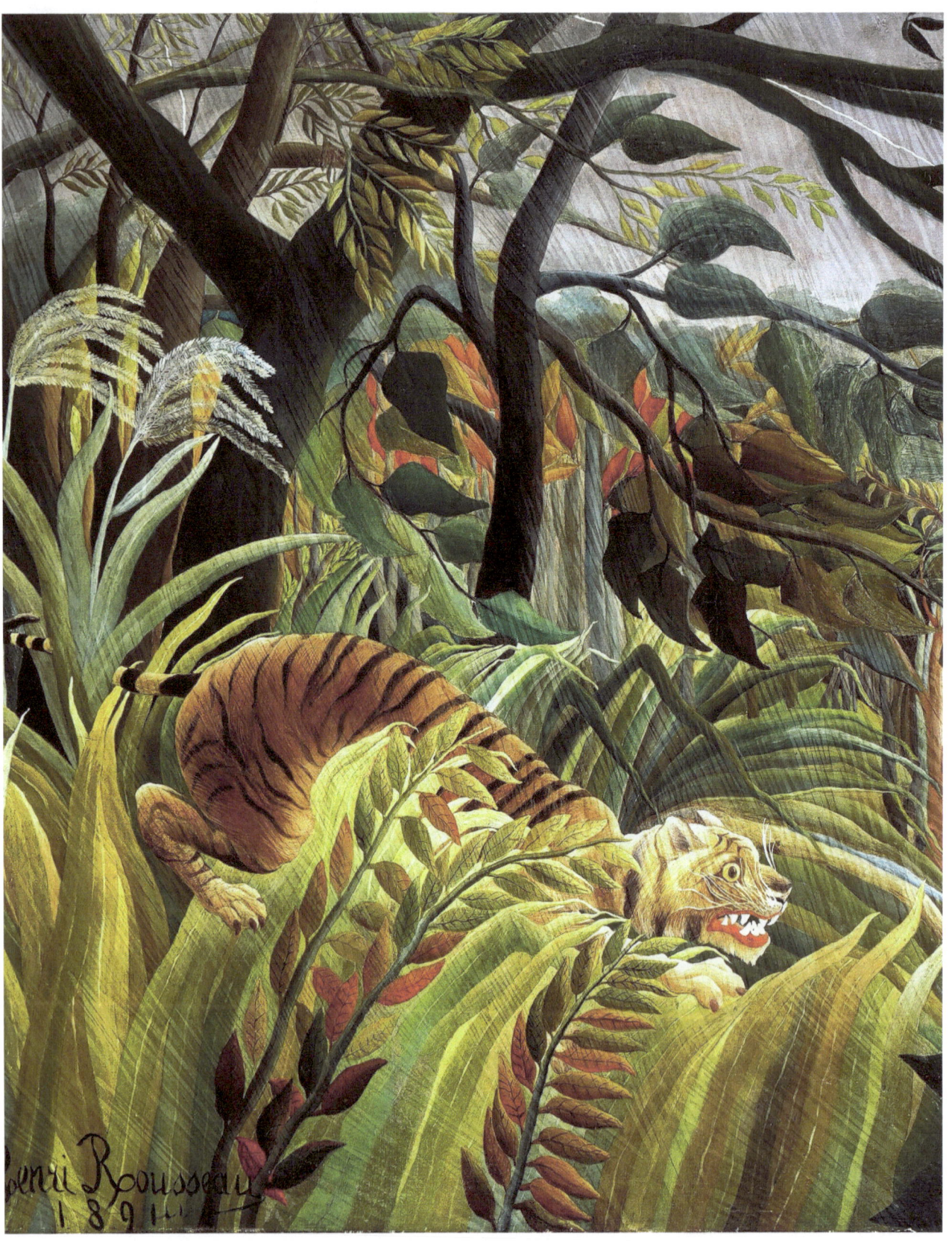

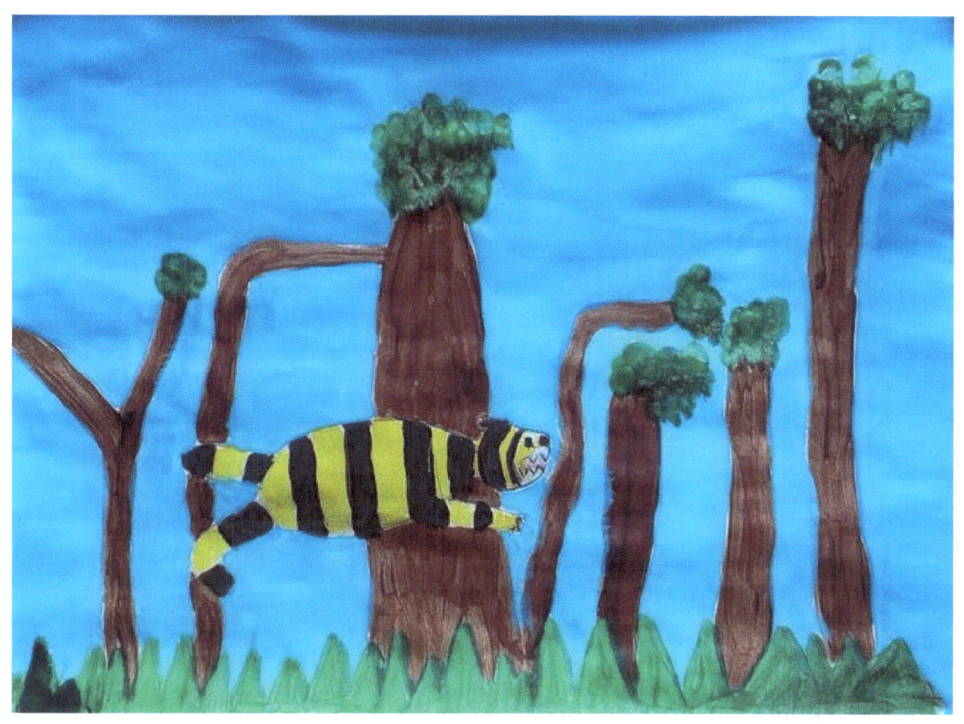

Jem aged 7 and Thom aged 10, showing their interpretations of The Surprise!

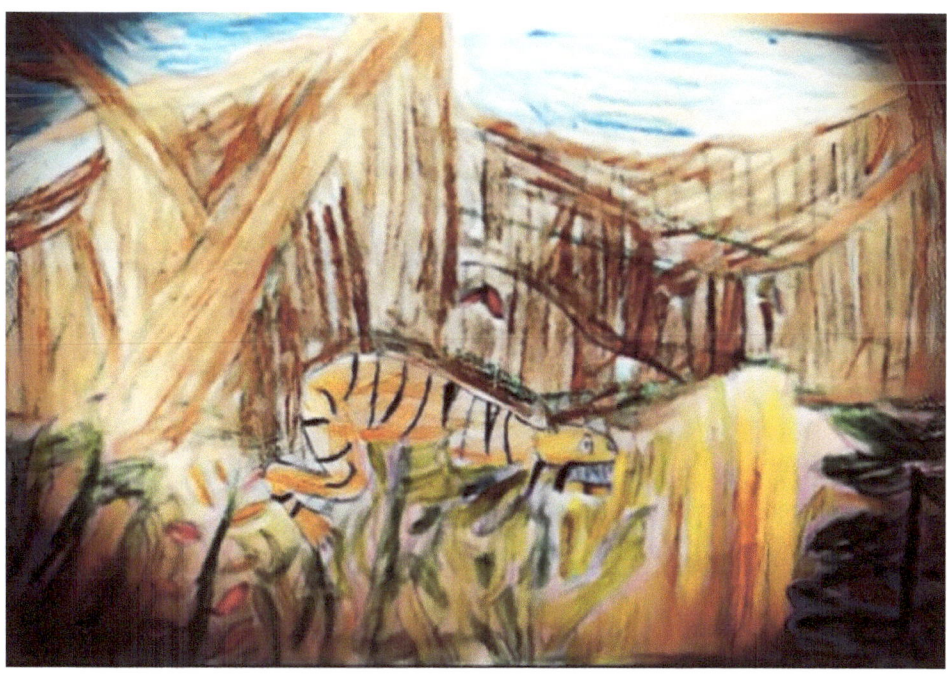

LUCY ANN LINNEY

I SPY FOXES

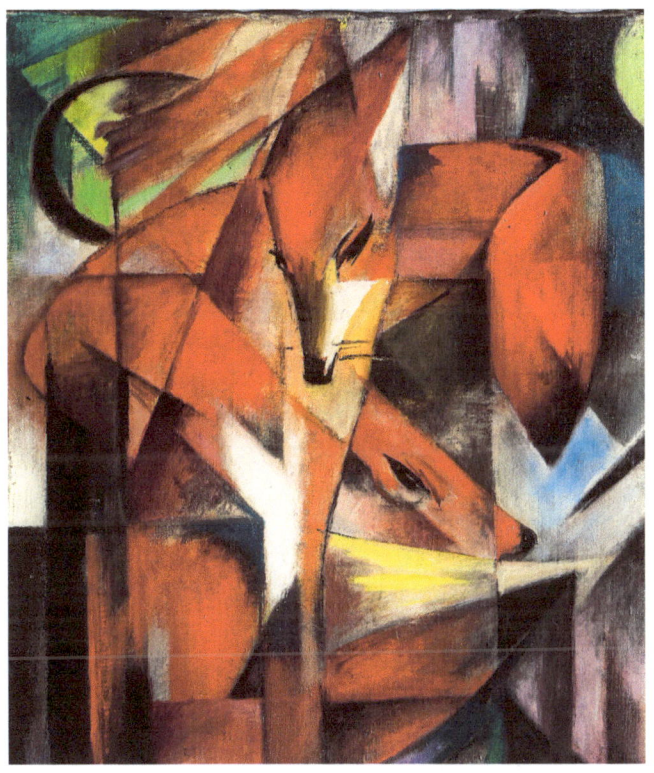

Artist: Franz Marc 1880 - 1916

Painting: The Foxes 1913

Held at The Museum Kunstpalast, Dusseldorf

A bright composition
with resounding harmony,
that grabs my attention
and fascinates me.
Like an electric fire
switched on in a room,
the red russet tones
dispel any gloom.
Bold, fiery colours
and hues rich and warm,
hit the right note
in kaleidoscope form.
A stained glass effect
from all angles seen,
fragmented and complex,
yet clear and serene.
Black eyes appear
away from the glare,
then noses and tails
in the camouflaged lair.
Foxes together,
coiled side by side,
at one with nature
concealed in their hide.
Surroundings may change,
thus staking their claim,
the beast and terrain
become one and the same.

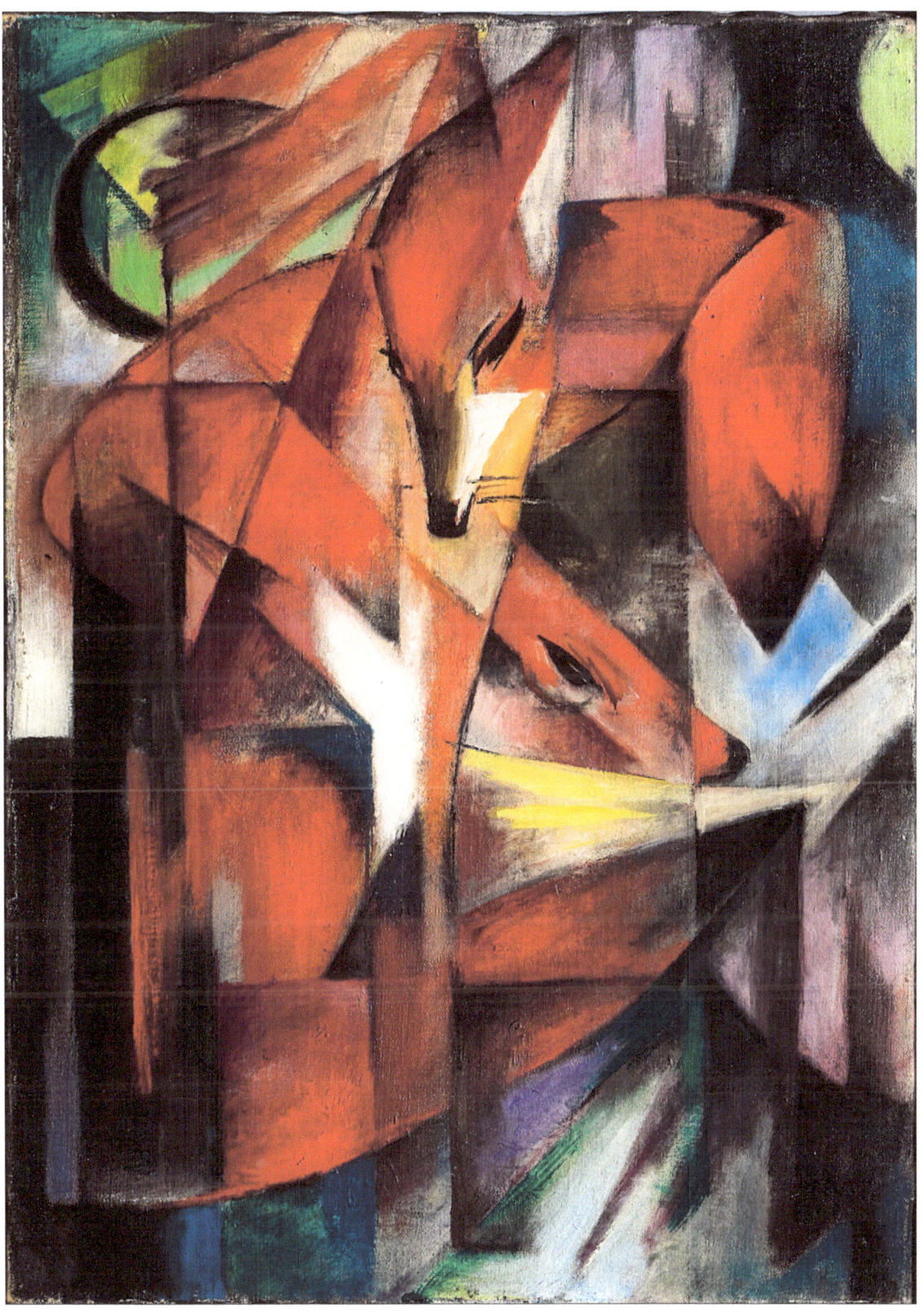

LUCY ANN LINNEY

MISTER COLOUR

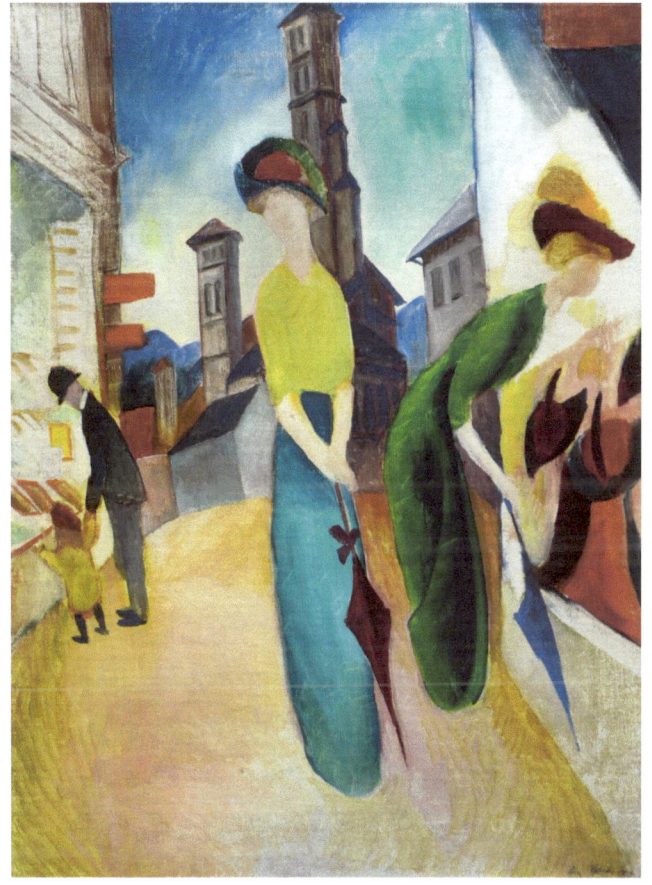

Artist: August Robert Ludwig Macke 1887 -1914

Painting: Two women before a hat shop 1913

Held at August - Macke -Haus, Bonn

Hello Mister Colour,
your nickname in the trade;
a master of expression
and gentle serenade.

Purity of sense and tone
engenders sympathy.
Works of art that show
Macke's own originality.

Situations commonplace,
in parks people are meeting.
Shoppers at the Mall
and in cafes, couples eating.

Gardens, streets, cathedrals
and a busy railway station,
ordinary subjects
fuelling our imagination.

Your friendship with Franz Marc,
in the exhibition phase,
spectacular and thrilling,
deserves the highest praise.

So sad your lives cut short
in the brutal first world war.
But you gave us lasting art
and left us wanting more.

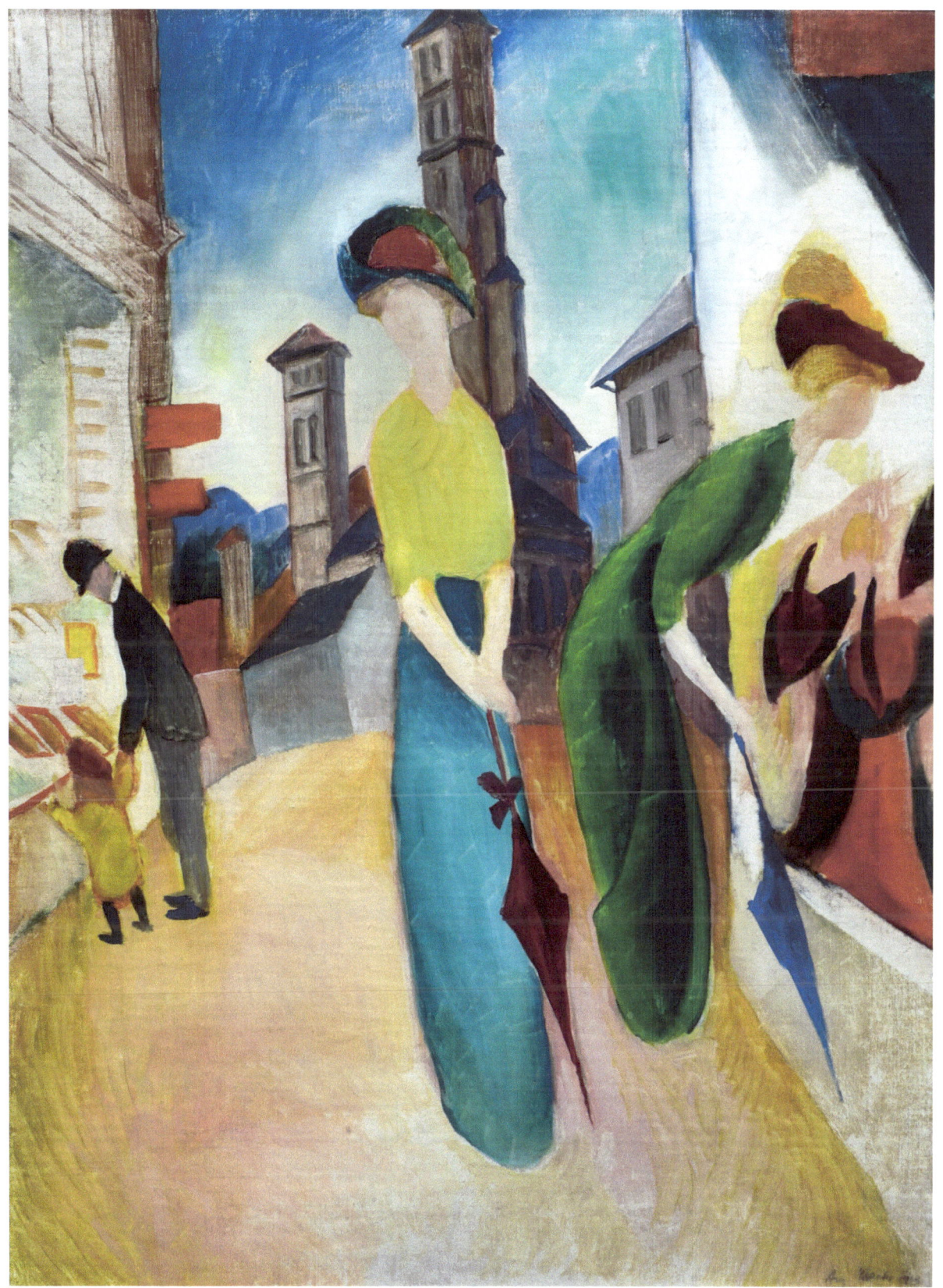

LUCY ANN LINNEY

ACKNOWLEDGEMENT

Alamy images with licence to publish:
ID TCBM4F   2AHY9GC   ID MHK3YA   ID MIYRDI   ID W7FP50
ID 2A8F2F8   ID RJRM68   ID 2D77HF3   ID DHXDE   ID T8H4K3
ID PW788E   Front Cover ID RJRM68

Thanks to my grandchildren:
Thom and Jem for their interpretations of Henri Rousseau's painting "The Surprise!" and to Harry for permission to use the photos of the lions in Trafalgar Square.
Thanks to my husband David for proof reading.

Select Bibliography:
Adventures of Odysseus: by Hugh Lupton, illustrated by Christina Balit
Art Journal: Feeling, Affect, Melancholy, Loss, Millais Autumn leaves and the Siege of Sebastopol by Kate Flint (Rutgers University Press)
Artists their lives and works: DK Penguin Random House
Casper David Friedrich: by Johannes Grave
David (Art and Ideas) Paperback by Simon Lee
Franz Marc and August Macke: 1909 -1914 by Vivian Endicott Barnett
Georges Seurat: 111 Paintings and Drawings by Maria Tsaneva
Henri Rousseau: Jungles in Paris by Christopher Green and Frances Morris
Jacques Louis David: by Anita Brooker and Maria Tsaneva
J.W. Waterhouse: by Peter Trippi
1001 Paintings you must see before you die: by Stephen Farthing
Pre-Raphaelites: Tate introductions by Jason Rosenfield
The letters of Vincent Van Gogh: selected and edited by Ronald De Leeuw Penguin Classic
The Monarch of the Glen: Landseer in the Highlands by Richard Louis Ormond and Edwin Landseer. Published by the trustees of National Galleries Scotland

ABOUT THE AUTHOR

Lucy Ann Linney

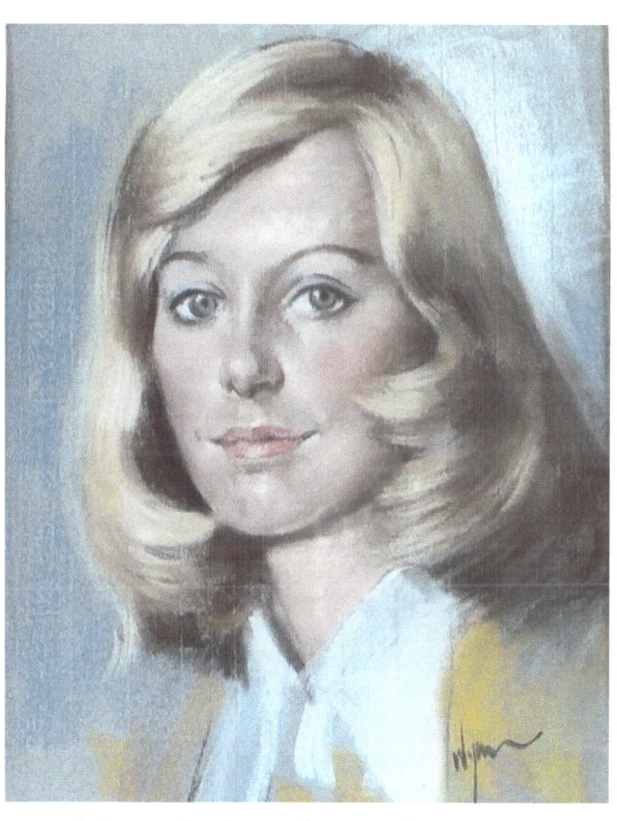

Lucy Ann Linney was born in 1949, the fourth of five children into a very musical family, steeped in church tradition and music.

She worked as a primary school teacher, when she was privileged to be involved in concerts at Wilden All Saints schoo, Wilden church and Kidderminster Town Hall.

Where in her words "The children were always the stars!"

She now lives with her husband David. They have twelve grandchildren between them.

Lockdown has meant less contact than one would like and so this book is dedicated to them.

Praise For The Author
Beauty in Picture and Rhyme:

I love how this book takes you through different styles of art, some well known and some not so well known. Lucy has a wonderful way with words that take you deep within the artwork to see the finer details.

It's like she takes a verbal brush that sweeps it's magic over the artwork to give it an extra dimension. This book is lovely to look at as well as lto read.

Jo jo G

BOOKS BY THIS AUTHOR

It's All About The Hat

This is the first poetry book in the series -
Poems about Famous Paintings and Artists.
The title is a nod to Paolo Uccello's work entitled The Battle of San Romano.
Here, the leader of the battle, Tolentino, is wearing a hat that is far too big and unsuitable for a battle. The poem questions why?
Other poems touch on how art may engender emotions in the observer. J.M.W. Turner's The Fighting Temeraire and Claude Monet's Impression Sunrise are just two brilliant examples.
Do you want to delve into art and find out more?
Through her poetry, Lucy Ann Linney has done a little light delving.

Dear Vincent

This poetry book contains an acknowledgement of Vincent Van Gogh's letters to his brother Theo and his sister Willemina, where Vincent talks about his time in Arles and the painting of The Cafe Terrace at Night.
The letters draw us into Vincent's world and the poem takes up the theme.
Lucy Ann Linney has unashamedly chosen ten more of her favourite paintings to continue the exploration of
 Famous Paintings and Artists, through poetry.

www.ingramcontent.com/pod-product-compliance
Lightning Source LLC
Chambersburg PA
CBHW051213220526
45473CB00003B/1016